Jobs at a Restaurant

Jobs

Vocabulary

restaurant [RES•tuh•rontl]
a place where people go to buy and eat a meal

chefs [SHEFS]
people who cook food at restaurants

cleaners [KLEEN•urz]
people who clean buildings

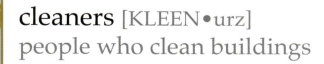

diners [DY•nurz]
people who eat at restaurants

dishes [DISH•uz]
things that food is served on

host [HOHST]
a person who greets people at a restaurant

order [OR•dur]
a request for something

server [SUR•vur]
a person who serves people in a reataurant

Lots of people work in restaurants.
Do you know what they do?
These are some jobs they do.

cooking food

cleaning

greeting guests

washing dishes

serving drinks

waiting tables

Who are these people?
What do they do
at the restaurant?
These people greet the diners.

Some people who greet diners, take the reservations.

Some people who greet diners, hand out menus.

greeting guests

restaurant owner

This woman is the host at the restaurant.

Who are these people?
They're servers.
What do they do
at the restaurant?
They take your order.
They bring your food.

bringing food

apron

tray

belt

bag

clearing tables

Who are these people?
They're chefs.
They cook the food
at the restaurant.

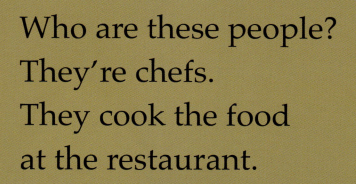

buying

preparing

marinating

cooking

cooking food

tasting

seasoning

plating

Who are these people?
What do they do?
They serve the drinks
at the restaurant.

This man is a wine server.

This woman makes coffee.

serving drinks

This woman brings water to the table.

Who are these people?
What do they do
at the restaurant?
These people wash the dishes.

pot

This man washes the pots.

This man stacks the clean dishes.

Who are these people?
They're cleaners.
They keep the restaurant clean and tidy.

This person stacks the chairs.

This person mops the floor.

cleaning

This person cleans the restaurant windows.

Some people do more than one job at a restaurant.

taking a reservation

drying glasses

putting up chairs

serving food

Job Advertisement

A job advertisement gives details of a position and the skills needed to get the job.

This job advertisement is for a chef.

CHEF

The Lake House Restaurant is looking for a qualified chef with at least five years experience in Mexican cuisine. The role is to develop new traditional Mexican-style meals for our already successful restaurant.
We require a team player with good communication skills who can work with little supervision in a busy kitchen.
Please apply in writing including details of experience and past employment history to Lake House Restaurant, 125 King Street, Brownton.
E-mail: headchef@lakehouse.com

Extra Vocabulary

apron
bag
belt
menu
napkin
tablecloth
tray

waiting tables

china bowl
dishwasher
plate
pot
steel bowl

washing dishes

buying
cooking
marinating
plating
preparing
seasoning
tasting

cooking food

Critical Thinking

- Which job do you think the person on pages 18–19 likes the best? Why?
- Which job requires the most skill?
- Which of her jobs would you most like to do?

Concepts: Jobs at a Restaurant

- There are different jobs that people do in restaurants.
- Some jobs involve working with diners.
- Some jobs are done by people that diners don't usually see.
- Some people do more than one job in a restaurant.